Images of Modern America

GETTYSBURG NATIONAL MILITARY PARK

The Gettysburg Battlefield is arguably one of the most photogenic sites in the nation. Here, a vibrant rainbow soars over the 6th New York Cavalry monument on Buford Avenue. (Author's collection.)

FRONT COVER: A cannon from Hazlett's Battery on Little Round Top. (Author's collection.)

UPPER BACK COVER: The Soldiers' National Cemetery on November 19, 2013. (Courtesy Buddy Secor.)

LOWER BACK COVER (from left to right): Reenactors of the "Liberty Rifles" march in the Remembrance Day Parade on November 20, 2010 (Author's collection.), Ranger John Nicholas guides a group past the Meade Monument (Courtesy GNMP.), Clark's Battery of the 1st New Jersey Light Artillery near the Peach Orchard (Courtesy Bill Dowling.)

Images of Modern America

GETTYSBURG NATIONAL MILITARY PARK

JARED FREDERICK
INTRODUCTION BY CHRISTOPHER GWINN

ARCADIA
PUBLISHING

Published by Arcadia Publishing
Charleston, South Carolina

Printed in the United States of America

Library of Congress Control Number: 2015954415

For all general information, please contact Arcadia Publishing:
Telephone 843-853-2070
Fax 843-853-0044
E-mail sales@arcadiapublishing.com
For customer service and orders:
Toll-Free 1-888-313-2665

Visit us on the Internet at www.arcadiapublishing.com

Dedicated to the memory of Stan O'Donnell:
licensed battlefield guide, Gettysburg authority, and friend

CONTENTS

Acknowledgments

What new can be said about Gettysburg? One of the most studied military confrontations in human history, the three-day struggle and subsequent address by Abraham Lincoln have come to represent epochal transitions of the national ideal. But the story does not end in 1863. Through this visual record, I seek to convey the ongoing history of the battlefield where this momentous clash of the Civil War took place. The book devotes particular attention to the profound role of the National Park Service and its stewardship of the landmark since the 1950s. With this book's release coinciding with the centennial of the National Park Service, now is a timely moment to reflect upon the people, strategies, and dramatic changes that continue to mold our perceptions of a turning point in history.

This project could not have been possible without the assistance of the staff and volunteers of Gettysburg National Military Park and Eisenhower National Historic Site, including Greg Goodell, John Heiser, John Joyce, Andrew Newman, and Evangelina Rubalcava Joyce. Management assistant Katie Lawhon provided invaluable help in procuring photographs while supervisory park ranger Christopher Gwinn was gracious enough to provide the introduction. I also wish to express gratitude to Scott Hartwig, Dr. Jen Murray, Barbara Sanders, and Cindy Small.

Finally, substantial credit is due to the various individuals whose works and collections grace the pages of this book: Barbara Adams, Garry Adelman, Jake Boritt, Erik Dorr, Bill Dowling, Jim Flook, Brad Graham, Patrick Gorman, Lynn Light Heller, John O'Grady, and Buddy Secor.

Courtesy lines and abbreviations are indicated by the following where applicable: Eisenhower National Historic Site (ENHS), Eisenhower Presidential Library (EPL), Gettysburg National Military Park (GNMP), and the National Park Service (NPS).

INTRODUCTION

On July 5, 1863, a team of photographers arrived on the still-smoldering battlefield at Gettysburg. They brought with them the innovative tools of their trade, transported in a mobile darkroom for the development of fragile glass-plate negatives. The three men—Alexander Gardner, Timothy O'Sullivan, and James F. Gibson—began the laborious and time-consuming process of capturing what they saw: images eventually to be reproduced, distributed, and sold. Altogether, they recorded over 50 unique negatives that conveyed the most immediate and visceral testimony pertaining to the Battle of Gettysburg.

By the time Gardner and company arrived, two days had passed since the battle's conclusion. The once-thriving town and surrounding countryside were scarred by the unmistakable signs of slaughter, chaos, and destruction. Formerly peaceful households were riddled with shot and shell while previously bucolic farms were ruined by the hard hand of war. The wounded and mangled spewed forth from every church, shack, and barn as burial parties embarked upon the task of digging shallow graves. As Gettysburg resident J. Howard Wert recalled, "No pen can paint the awful picture of desolation, devastation, and death that was presented here to the shuddering beholders. . . . It was a hideous and revolting sight."

Over the ensuing years, Gettysburg struggled to overcome the carnage and devastation inflicted in 1863. In many respects, the community never recovered. The photographic record of the enterprising artists of the time permits us to partly comprehend the challenges of soldiers and civilians. These photographs, and others taken over the following 150 years, allow us to describe the indescribable and decipher the indecipherable. The images are simultaneously a by-product of creative expression and invaluable tools of historical understanding.

Casting light on events and lives of the past, photographs allow us to walk in the theoretical footsteps of our predecessors. They capture moments beautiful and transcendent as well as episodes dark and painful. Visual records spare these episodes from the inevitable evaporation that befalls so many historical events through the passing of time.

Much of the 1863 battlefield is today preserved within the nearly 7,000 acres of Gettysburg National Military Park. Contemporary visitors will find little outward vestige of the true horrors inflicted by the armies during the American Civil War. Rather, they encounter a well-maintained park, a quaint downtown, and a hauntingly serene pastoral landscape. Above all else, the battlefield remains a place of pilgrimage and remembrance for millions of individuals from every corner of the world.

Stoic monuments and markers dot the landscape where armed combatants once waged a desperate struggle for the future of a nation. Temporary muddy graves have been replaced by granite stones in the Soldiers' National Cemetery to denote the sacrifices. Meanwhile, Abraham Lincoln's venerated words of consecration have been transmuted into bronze. The landscape continues to beckon and inspire modern Americans in dramatic ways. In this sense, photographs from the 20th and 21st centuries serve as significant forms of historical reflection. Gettysburg's vibrant heritage is a never-ending tale of how we seek to connect with those who have gone before us.

Historian Jared Frederick, himself intimately connected to the Gettysburg Battlefield as a former park ranger, has scoured the park archives and other collections for images of the famous and not-so-famous moments that have defined the present-day battlefield. His efforts have yielded a fascinating collection of photographs and commentary that chronicle the broad scope of the park's evolution since the bustling tourism days of the 1950s. Analyzing the baby boomer era through the battle's 2013 sesquicentennial, readers will be treated to a visual chronology of Gettysburg National Military Park's continual transformations. Most importantly, the images on the following pages highlight the ways in which the national park has been commemorated, celebrated, defined, and redefined throughout the ages.

Chapter one explores various episodes of park history from the 1950s through the 1990s, when battlefield visitation skyrocketed. The second chapter examines snapshots of the visitor experience in more recent years. The book's subsequent section studies the dramatic changes brought forth through landscape restoration while the final chapter marks the 150th anniversary of the battle.

Denoting the contributions and observances of staff and visitors from all walks of life, the visuals presented in these chapters are a mosaic of America's most visited battlefield. Much like Alexander Gardner's 1863 negatives, the photographs here elicit the alluring power of Gettysburg and its centrality to our national story. As the National Park Service celebrates its 100th anniversary, these images serve as a timely reminder of the many meanings and emotions Gettysburg evokes.

—Christopher Gwinn
Supervisory Park Ranger
Gettysburg National Military Park

From left to right, park rangers Scott Hartwig, Jared Frederick, Chris Gwinn, Dan Vermilya, and Philip Brown gather after the 150th commemoration of Pickett's Charge on July 3, 2013. (Author's collection.)

One

HISTORY BOOM

In the post–World War II era, the baby boom, the ease of family travel, a burgeoning economy, and patriotism drove Americans to their national parks at an unprecedented rate. Here, Ray Middleton portrays the 16th president in the program "Lincoln Comes to Gettysburg," the finale of the Western Maryland Railroad's centennial on October 19, 1952. (Courtesy GNMP.)

Gettysburg has long hosted ceremonial pageantry evoking the military tradition. Here, from left to right, Spanish–American War signalmen Arthur Lowe, Warren Jacobus, and Henry Wells present their flag to Lt. Col. Gordon Beach at Little Round Top's Signal Corps marker on July 4, 1950, to honor veterans from the Civil War and beyond. (Courtesy GNMP.)

Marking Lincoln's birthday, some 5,000 Boy Scouts paraded into the snowy grounds of Soldiers' National Cemetery on February 12, 1953. The Scouts listened to patriotic speeches, sang "God Bless America," and then proceeded to campfire lunches. Scouts frequently utilize the battlefield to promote civic awareness. (Courtesy GNMP.)

In 1950, Gettysburg National Military Park (GNMP) welcomed unlikely neighbors in the form of Dwight "Ike" Eisenhower and his wife, Mamie. Fresh from victory in Europe, Ike yearned to own a patch of land and cultivate it. He and Mamie are seen here in front of their new home on their wedding anniversary on July 1, 1955—the same anniversary as the Battle of Gettysburg. (EPL photograph; courtesy ENHS.)

Following the 1952 election, Eisenhower's 189-acre farm became a showpiece of his presidency. He boasted of the property's rich Civil War history and strived to maintain the pastoral environment. He also prided himself on his Angus cattle and barbecuing skills. Eisenhower is seen here with his trusted valet, M.Sgt. John Moaney. (EPL photograph; courtesy ENHS.)

Eisenhower (left) was an avid history buff and actively turned to the past for insight. Accordingly, Ike readily treated guests to battlefield tours. One such excursion that gained notoriety was World War II general Bernard Montgomery's May 12, 1957, visit. "Monty" (center) created a public relations fiasco when he harshly critiqued Generals Lee and Meade's military performances. (EPL photograph; courtesy ENHS.)

On April 24, 1960, Eisenhower (center) welcomed French president Charles de Gaulle (left) to Gettysburg to discuss Cold War policies. Despite political tensions in the past, the two former generals relished the opportunity to talk military strategy. In analyzing the actions of Lee and Meade, de Gaulle observed, "Victory often goes to the army that makes the least mistakes, not the most brilliant plans." (EPL photograph; courtesy ENHS.)

Serving as vice president under Eisenhower, Richard Nixon visited Gettysburg on several occasions. Interestingly, the future president's great-grandfather, George Nixon, of the 73rd Ohio Infantry, was mortally wounded at Gettysburg. On July 5, 1953, Nixon placed a bouquet at his forbearer's gravestone. Shown are, from left to right, Dr. E.L. Nixon, ranger J.W.L. Riddle, Congressman Walter Stauffer, Mayor W.G. Weaver, Nixon, and John Basehore. (Courtesy GNMP.)

Gettysburg was designated a national park in 1895. Ever since, the battlefield has flourished as an outdoor classroom for the leaders of tomorrow. On October 8, 1954, Marine Corps officers from Quantico, Virginia, toured the field and examined Union artillery at the Angle, the site at which Pickett's Charge was repulsed on July 3, 1863. (Courtesy GNMP.)

Acclaimed poet and Lincoln author Carl Sandburg (left) meets with Hon. Arthur Fleming (center) and park historian Fred Tilberg (right) at the Soldiers' National Monument on November 19, 1959, in preparation for the 96th anniversary of the Gettysburg Address. So moving was Sandburg's rendition of Lincoln's speech, the *Gettysburg Times* reported a serene stillness and many spectators in tears. (Courtesy GNMP.)

As interest in the Civil War expanded with the approach of the conflict's centennial, park leaders realized their lack of proper visitor facilities required improvement. A modernist design by Austrian-born architect Richard Neutra (front center) was dedicated on Cemetery Ridge as a contemporary visitor center and memorial to Lincoln on November 19, 1962. (Courtesy GNMP.)

As part of Mission 66—the comprehensive effort of national parks to prepare for the National Park Service (NPS) semicentennial—Gettysburg oversaw construction of its new visitor center to accommodate the mammoth cyclorama painting of Pickett's Charge in "the drum" at right. Visitors ascended a spiral walkway to the presentation upstairs. The base of the drum featured battle debris, dioramas, and exhibits. (Courtesy GNMP.)

The "Battle of Gettysburg" cyclorama was the IMAX of its day. The massive 360-degree painting of Pickett's Charge by French artist Paul Philippoteaux was completed in 1884 and premiered in Gettysburg in 1913. In the 1962 visitor center, a sound and light show followed by ranger commentary dramatized the battle. Later, a program narrated by celebrated actor Richard Dreyfuss was installed. (Courtesy GNMP.)

Driving from nearby Camp David on March 31, 1963, Pres. John F. Kennedy and First Lady Jackie Kennedy were treated to a battlefield tour by local history teacher Jacob Sheads (back to the camera), as seen here on Little Round Top. A lifelong student of history, Kennedy was moved by his visit. By year's end, Gettysburg's Eternal Peace Light Memorial became the inspiration for JFK's eternal flame at Arlington National Cemetery. (Courtesy Gettysburg Museum of History.)

Vice Pres. Lyndon B. Johnson and daughter Luci spent Memorial Day 1963 in Gettysburg. Delivering a profound speech foreshadowing the Civil Rights Act, LBJ noted, "One hundred years ago, the slave was freed. One hundred years later, the Negro remains in bondage to the color of his skin." America had "fallen short of assuring freedom to the free." (Courtesy Gettysburg Museum of History.)

The civil rights struggle was reflected at Gettysburg's centennial commemoration at the Eternal Peace Light Memorial on July 1, 1963. Twenty-nine governors attended. New Jersey governor Richard Hughes argued, "It is our shame at this moment that the full benefits of freedom are not in the possession of all Americans, a full century after the war which was fought to save America's soul." (Courtesy GNMP.)

In a symbolic moment of harmony, Gov. Endicott Peabody of Massachusetts (left) and Gov. Karl Rolvaag of Minnesota (center) placed a wreath at the Virginia Memorial alongside Robert E. Lee IV on July 2, 1963. Also present at various ceremonies was segregationist Alabama governor George Wallace, who warned the *Gettysburg Times*, "[W]e are traveling down the dead-end road of destructive centralization." (Courtesy GNMP.)

The 1963 Gettysburg commemoration was steeped in the traditions of Lost Cause mythology—minimalizing the historical roles of race and slavery while promoting postwar national unity. Above, Confederate reenactors re-create Pickett's Charge with stereophonic sound effects rather than actual black powder. Union reenactors shook hands with the Southerners at the program's finale. (Courtesy GNMP.)

This view from July 3, 1963, reveals new urban sprawl along Steinwehr Avenue at right, Soldiers' National Cemetery at left, and overflow parking for centennial observances. The *Gettysburg Times* remarked, "The re-enactment took a good many liberties with history but many of the visitors seemed to think afterwards it was a good show." (Courtesy GNMP.)

The Gettysburg centennial gained national recognition and was featured on a US Postal Service stamp. However, many national leaders of the centennial sought to make commemorations commercialized celebrations. As one *Holiday* magazine editorial complained, the nation was celebrating the conflict in "holiday mood . . . cheered on by the gleeful commercial interests and blessed sentimentalists" who romanticized the war. (Courtesy National Postal Museum.)

Few individuals had greater influence on the Civil War centennial than Dwight Eisenhower (left) and acclaimed writer Bruce Catton (right)—both seen here at the High Water Mark for a Lincoln documentary. "The principles of war," Ike said, "are the principles of life fulfilled whenever an individual has a task." (EPL photograph; courtesy ENHS.)

On November 19, 1963, dignitaries convened to mark the centenary of the Gettysburg Address. Dwight Eisenhower stands at the podium, and famed singer Marian Anderson stands at left. Due to a program error, Anderson required a hymnal. One was quickly acquired at nearby St. James Church. It was inscribed, "To Marian Anderson, whose ministry of song has inspired millions." (Courtesy GNMP.)

From left to right, park ranger Dr. Frederick Tilberg (1895–1979) interacts with Soviet war hero Konstantin Ivanovich Serov, interpreter Vladimir Smirnov, and author Sergy Smirnov at Arnold's Battery on May 30, 1961. Hired as an assistant historian in 1937, Dr. Tilberg is considered one of the godfathers of historical interpretation at Gettysburg. The ranger continually advocated educational programs for public benefit, initiating a long-standing tradition. (Courtesy GNMP.)

Park ranger Harry Pfanz began his career at Gettysburg in 1956. Wounded in the Battle of the Bulge, Pfanz had an intimate understanding of warfare and later conveyed those insights as park historian. Following his 1981 retirement, he crafted a celebrated in-depth trilogy on Gettysburg. Pfanz passed away in 2015 at age 93. (Courtesy GNMP.)

On June 18, 1966, the Arkansas Monument was dedicated on West Confederate Avenue. Despite amicable remarks by its dedicators, the monument itself suggests an existing tension between North and South. The figure being trampled in the lower left of the monument bears suspicious resemblance to Abraham Lincoln. (Courtesy GNMP.)

In July 1968, World War I veterans of Gettysburg's Camp Colt convened to mark the 50th anniversary of the war. The delegation is seen here at the park's amphitheater on West Confederate Avenue. The site of Dwight Eisenhower's first military command, Camp Colt trained some 15,000 doughboys during the conflict. (Courtesy GNMP.)

A standard staple of interpretation at Gettysburg is the "Civil War Soldier" presentation. A 1960s rendition of this program can be seen here outside the Bryan Farm. After watching the cyclorama program inside the nearby visitor center, tourists exited the building to watch a period-clad ranger conduct weapons demonstrations. (Courtesy GNMP.)

The battlefield often serves as a public forum to discuss momentous cultural issues. As part of the nationwide Moratorium Day to end the Vietnam War on October 15, 1969, hundreds of Gettysburg College students (standing to the right of the camera) marched and sang to the Eternal Peace Light Memorial to protest American involvement in Southeast Asia. (Courtesy GNMP.)

Even while Vietnam dramatically divided the nation, Americans nonetheless continued to find resonance in Abraham Lincoln's visions for unity. Citizens and the Gettysburg High School Band gathered at the Soldiers' National Monument on November 19, 1968. Organized by the Lincoln Fellowship of Pennsylvania, these Dedication Days have grown in scale and prominence. (Courtesy GNMP.)

In Zeigler's Grove stands a monument to the Grand Army of the Republic and its last soldier, Albert Woolson. The veteran died in 1956 but did not fight at Gettysburg. At this November 22, 1969, Sons of Union Veterans ceremony, Gen. W.A. Morgan likened the tumult of the 1960s to the 1860s. He beseeched Americans to support President Nixon so victory in Vietnam could be won "with honor." (Courtesy GNMP.)

On February 11, 1970, the park celebrated its 75th birthday with a reception. The visitor center open house from 10:00 a.m. to 9:00 p.m. included free showings of the cyclorama and orientation film. According to the *Gettysburg Times*, over 1,150 people toured the building, leaving Supt. George Emery "well pleased." Pictured are, from left to right, park staff members Alice Mathews, Carmen Doyle, and Joyce Staley. (Courtesy GNMP.)

Walter Cronkite (left center), Mamie Eisenhower (right center), and Pennsylvania governor Raymond Shafer (right) gathered at Meade's headquarters on September 12, 1970. This ceremony unveiled "The Final Fury," a cassette tour based on the works of Bruce Catton, narrated by Cronkite, and produced by CBS. Over 500 people attended the ceremony, at which Cronkite encouraged society to learn from its mistakes so it could "move forward in peace." (Courtesy GNMP.)

One of three Gettysburg statues sculpted by Donald De Lue, the Mississippi Monument was dedicated on October 18, 1973. The statue barely arrived in time. Cast in Italy, the bronze art was delayed by an Italian dockworkers strike. Upon its arrival in America, the truck transporting the memorial broke down in New Jersey. The statue was installed at 8:10 p.m. the day before its dedication. (Courtesy GNMP.)

Among the legendary tourist attractions of Gettysburg was the Electric Map. Built in the privately owned Gettysburg National Museum in 1939 by the Rosensteel family, the large map featured lightbulbs representing troop movements. This photograph re-creation shows the map similar to its 1940s appearance. The NPS assumed operation of the museum in 1973. (Courtesy Historical Films.)

On June 26, 1976, the Diocese of Harrisburg held a memorial Mass at the Eternal Peace Light Memorial to celebrate the national bicentennial. Over 500 people attended the service, in which the monument was converted into a large altar. Bishop George Leech sermonized, "The unity of America is forever associated with Gettysburg." Here, "Americans finally sealed our destiny under God as a free and united people." (Courtesy GNMP.)

Indicative of the energy and environmental crises of the 1970s, Gettysburg's eternal flame was converted from gas to electric on July 1, 1978. From left to right, Mrs. Paul Roy, Ron Nicodemus, Secretary of the Interior Cecil Andrus, and Supt. John Earnst threw the switch for the memorial relighting. (Courtesy GNMP.)

On September 9, 1978, Pres. Jimmy Carter (center) brought Israeli prime minister Menachem Begin (left of Carter) and Egyptian president Anwar al Sadat (right of Carter) to the battlefield during the Camp David Accords. Carter successfully utilized Gettysburg as an analogy to ongoing Mideast struggles. Below, ranger Bob Prosperi speaks to the delegation at the Soldiers' National Monument. Israeli minister of foreign affairs Moshe Dayan can be seen wearing his eye patch at left. (Courtesy GNMP.)

As the national bicentennial helped reignite interest in history, the interpretive staff of Gettysburg implemented creative educational techniques. The Slyder Farm became a living history station where visitors could learn about 19th-century agricultural life. Unfortunately, few visitors strayed from the main tour route, and the Slyder Farm project was short-lived. (Courtesy GNMP.)

Throngs of visitors poured into Gettysburg for the battle's 125th anniversary. Among them was 70-year-old Col. Allen Nelson of Samford, Florida. Nelson's father, George Harvey Nelson, was a teenage recruit of the 2nd Vermont Infantry, which participated at Gettysburg. Allen was born when his father was 72. In this photograph, Nelson traces the footsteps of his dad's regiment. (Courtesy GNMP.)

At the stone wall where Pickett's Charge was turned back 125 years prior, Pennsylvania governor Robert Casey and Virginia governor Gerald Baliles exchanged historical flags for display in the park museum. Baliles unveiled the regimental flag of the 18th Virginia Infantry, while Casey presented a state banner made in Philadelphia for the dedication of the Soldiers' National Cemetery. (Courtesy GNMP.)

On July 3, 1863, a Confederate projectile struck the barrel of this cannon of the 1st Rhode Island Light Artillery. When the Federal cannoneers tried firing back, their own ball became wedged in the muzzle. For the 125th anniversary, this famed cannon was brought 400 miles from the Rhode Island State House for display at Gettysburg. (Courtesy GNMP.)

A 90-by-45-foot flag from Mount Rushmore was displayed for the Eternal Peace Light Memorial rededication on July 3, 1988. Dr. Carl Sagan (at podium) spoke of peace, unaware that the United States shot down an Iranian airliner that same day. Sagan noted the next morning, "The history of the human species is a battle between education and disaster." However, "our ability to commit gruesome and global scale annihilation increases every day." (Courtesy GNMP.)

Flags played a prominent thematic role in the 125th anniversary of Gettysburg. These 9-by-20-foot "Peace Flags" with 34 stars adorned the grounds of Oak Hill. As the *Gettysburg Times* reported, "Those unable to find shade [under the flags] used suntan lotion and took advantage of the beautiful weather and sunbathed." (Courtesy GNMP.)

Mock battles are prohibited in national parks in the effort to maintain the physical and historical integrity of battlefields. On July 3, 1988, however, an unplanned "rogue reenactment" took place on the fields of Pickett's Charge in which rangers helplessly watched a re-creation of the assault. Here, unsupervised reenactors unknowingly erode original earthworks by marching over them. (Courtesy GNMP.)

On a drizzly November 19, 1988, Chief Justice William Rehnquist joined thousands in Soldiers' National Cemetery to mark the 125th anniversary of the Gettysburg Address. In his remarks, Rehnquist referred to Lincoln's words as "the purest gold of human eloquence." (Courtesy GNMP.)

In November 1988, locals welcomed eight unlikely guests from the Soviet Union. Russian mayors traveled to Gettysburg in preparation for a student exchange program as a Cold War goodwill initiative. Here, Supt. Daniel Kuehn attempts to explain Lincoln's vision of democracy to Communists. (Courtesy GNMP.)

Throughout the summer of 1992, filmmakers of the movie *Gettysburg* obtained unprecedented access to the battlefield, as is shown in this scene filmed at the Slyder Farm. From left to right are actors Pat Falci, Warren Burton, Patrick Gorman, Tom Berenger, Ivan Kane, and Les Kinsolving. (Courtesy Patrick Gorman.)

Actors Tom Berenger (left center) and James Lancaster (right center) prepare for a scene filmed near the Slyder Farm on the set of *Gettysburg*. Director Ron Maxwell (far right) struggled for over a decade to produce and finance the production. The movie enlisted the expertise of thousands of volunteer reenactors to stage massive battle scenes. (Courtesy Patrick Gorman.)

Gettysburg director Ron Maxwell prepares to shoot a scene with Martin Sheen. The movie debuted strongly in theaters in October 1993. When the feature aired as a TNT miniseries in the summer of 1994, nearly 40 million viewers tuned in. The movie helped fuel interest in the Civil War and brought a new generation of visitors to the park. (Courtesy Patrick Gorman.)

The movie *Gettysburg* had a substantial impact on Americans' perceptions of the Civil War and led to a boom in reenacting. This view shows Federal reenactors deploying at the 2008 Gettysburg Anniversary Reenactment north of town. Contrary to popular belief, these re-creations are not held on the actual battlefield or affiliated with the NPS. (Author's collection.)

In 1973, the former Gettysburg National Museum became the park's new visitor center. The neighboring Cyclorama Center proved inadequate to handle large numbers of visitors on its own. By the 1990s, the two facilities still struggled to properly accommodate droves of tourists. Additionally, the dated museum's valuable artifact collection lacked historical context and proper storage. (Courtesy GNMP.)

In the lobby of the former visitor center, guests could obtain park literature, buy tickets to the Electric Map presentation, or schedule a private tour with a licensed battlefield guide. To the left was the park bookstore. Beyond the lobby was the entrance to the cavernous, homespun museum. From spring through fall, this lobby was constantly filled to capacity. (Courtesy GNMP.)

While the NPS was confined with its indoor space, outdoor programs flourished. In-depth "Battlewalks" were first proposed by park rangers such as Gregory Coco (1946–2009), seen here with troops in Soldiers' National Cemetery. Today, these programs are offered daily during the summer and continually attract dedicated audiences. (Courtesy GNMP.)

By the 2000s, new educational initiatives included specialized programs for middle schoolers. Above, educational specialist Barbara Sanders guides youngsters through the fields of Pickett's Charge. Other methods incorporated into scholastic endeavors included the "Traveling Trunk" program, in which reproduction Civil War items and learning materials were shipped to schools throughout the nation. Through effective distance learning, students can experience Gettysburg even if they cannot visit in person. (Courtesy GNMP.)

Ranger Tom Holbrook encourages an enthusiastic group of students at the Angle. Park rangers have long recognized that battlefield experiences such as these are fundamental to any visitor. However, in order to effectively reach out to millennials and youth, sweeping changes were under way that would dramatically alter the park and its strategies. (Courtesy GNMP.)

Two

VISITORS AND VISTAS

The pristine nature of the Gettysburg Battlefield makes it one of the most photogenic historic sites in the world. Here, a vibrant sunset shines over the guns of Clark's Battery of the 1st New Jersey Light Artillery near the Peach Orchard. The guns positioned here on July 2, 1863, were involved in five hours of combat and fired over 1,300 rounds at Confederates. (Courtesy Bill Dowling.)

Among the best times to visit Gettysburg is the winter season. Tourism congestion is less and a lack of vegetation allows visitors to better distinguish key terrain features, including 1860s earthworks. Above, Confederate artillery stands vigilant near the Henry Spangler Farm. (Courtesy GNMP.)

The family of African American Abraham Bryan resided on this farmstead until Confederate invasion temporarily made them fleeing refugees. Interestingly, Federal soldiers used part of Bryan's stone wall to repulse Pickett's Charge. Like many Gettysburg families, the Bryans unsuccessfully put forth a government compensation claim after the battle. They filed for $1,028 but received only $15. Even so, their freedom was preserved. (Courtesy Lynn Light Heller.)

The monument to the 1st Minnesota Infantry is one of the most iconic in the park. Engaged in a desperate charge on Cemetery Ridge, the unit was hurled at a Confederate force four times larger than its own. Some 215 of the 262 men in the regiment were struck down throughout the battle—an astounding 82 percent casualty rate. (Courtesy Lynn Light Heller.)

One of the most visited locations at Gettysburg is the Angle, the breaking point of Pickett's Charge. Associated with the turning point of the Civil War, this ground has acquired a mythical aura. Monuments such as the 72nd Pennsylvania Infantry monument silhouetted against the sunset offer a sense of serenity in stark comparison to the carnage inflicted here. (Buddy Secor photograph; courtesy GNMP.)

Visitors from all walks of life are drawn to Gettysburg for increasingly diverse reasons. Beyond its historical connotations, the battlefield is a haven for artists, photographers, and nature lovers. In March 2015, the park teamed with the National Parks Arts Foundation to host artist residencies on the battlefield. (Buddy Secor photograph; courtesy GNMP.)

Stunning scenery can be found even amid the cold grayness of Pennsylvania winters. In this sunset image, the 7th West Virginia Infantry monument stands vigil on Cemetery Hill—the key position for the Union army. (Courtesy Lynn Light Heller.)

Small tokens of affection are frequently left at monuments in memory of Civil War soldiers. This bouquet was left at the foot of the 83rd Pennsylvania Infantry monument on Little Round Top in the name of Pvt. Philip Grine. The enlisted man died after being shot in the abdomen on July 2, 1863. He was 21 years of age. (Author's collection.)

On September 5, 2008, Pres. George W. Bush (third from right) and First Lady Laura Bush (third from left) toured the battlefield with historian Gabor Boritt (second from right) and documentarian Jake Boritt (pointing). The unofficial presidential visit from Camp David also included adviser Karl Rove and Karen Hughes of the US Department of State (far left). Only days later, the onset of the 2008 economic recession ensued. (Courtesy Jake Boritt.)

Since 2006, the Sgt. Mac Foundation has overseen the placement of Christmas wreaths on the tombstones of service members at Quantico and Gettysburg. John and Susan McColley of Gettysburg initiated the undertaking in memory of their son, Sgt. Eric McColley, who was killed in a helicopter crash off the coast of Africa on February 17, 2006. (Courtesy GNMP.)

On March 24, 2009, Holmes Cycling and Fitness of Camp Hill, Pennsylvania, donated three new bicycles to the law enforcement team of Gettysburg National Military Park. Seen here, from left to right, rangers John Sherman, Maria Brady, and Doug Murphy test their newly acquired patrol gear at the Pennsylvania monument. (Courtesy GNMP.)

Every May, Gettysburg welcomes a new batch of interns and summer employees to present tours and orientation. One facet of their training included a "History March" in period clothing to gain a sense of 1860s life. From left to right are (first row, kneeling) Scott Hartwig and Jared Frederick; (second row, standing) Rich Smith, Glenn Knight, Matt Atkinson, Dan Welch, Kristen Campbell, Bob Hall, and Chris Brusatte preparing for their 2009 hike. (Author's collection.)

A compelling tradition at Gettysburg is the oath of citizenship ceremony that occurs on the anniversary of the Gettysburg Address. Celebrating the American process, the November 19, 2009, ceremony seen here possessed special significance as it marked Lincoln's birthday bicentennial year. The keynote speaker was actor Richard Dreyfuss, who heralded civics education and tolerance. (Courtesy GNMP.)

Not all park visitors embrace equality as proclaimed in the Gettysburg Address. On Juneteenth (a holiday celebrating slavery's abolishment) in 2010, the Aryan Nations—a white supremacist organization—held a rally near the former Cyclorama Center to condemn immigrants and homosexuals. Counter protesters stood nearby with banners exclaiming, "All you need is love." Regardless of rhetoric, all citizens are free to exercise First Amendment rights on public lands. (Courtesy GNMP.)

Park staff was greeted by a visit by First Lady Michelle Obama on September 1, 2010. Accompanied by daughters Malia and Sasha, the first lady was guided on a low-key battlefield tour. Pictured before the tour are, from left to right, chief ranger Brion Fitzgerald, educational specialist Barbara Sanders, Michelle Obama, Barbara Finfrock of the Gettysburg Foundation, and Supt. Bob Kirby. (Courtesy GNMP.)

In the fall of 2010, director Brad Graham of Historical Films produced a special educational documentary for youth entitled *You Are a Soldier*. The film was meant to compliment the park's highly successful "Traveling Trunk" program by illustrating the daily routines of Civil War soldiers. The cast of the documentary is shown on set at the Rose Farm. (Courtesy Historical Films.)

D. Scott Hartwig emerged as one of the most notable park rangers at Gettysburg. Gaining employment with the NPS at the newly created Eisenhower National Historic Site in 1980, he rose through the ranks to become the battlefield's supervisory historian, a position he popularly held until his 2014 retirement. Hartwig is seen here during "Taps" in Soldiers' National Cemetery on November 19, 2010. (Author's collection.)

A popular component of the ceremonies associated with the anniversary of the Gettysburg Address is the Remembrance Day Parade. Thousands of reenactors proceed through the historic downtown, including the authentically clad "Liberty Rifles," shown here on Steinwehr Avenue on November 20, 2010. (Author's collection.)

The annual Remembrance Day Parade is hosted by the Sons of Union Veterans, a fraternal organization that carries on the work of Civil War veterans. Living historian Stan McGee (far left with sword) is seen here on November 19, 2011, leading reenactors representing the 5th New York Infantry, an iconic Zouave unit. (Author's collection.)

As part of the America the Beautiful initiative, the US Mint chose a 72nd Pennsylvania Infantry monument representation for a Gettysburg quarter. Ironically, many Union veterans despised this memorial, as they felt the regiment's members politicked to have it erected in a prominent but inaccurate spot. Almost poetically to some, the memorial fell over during a June 2013 windstorm, mangling it for the battle's 150th anniversary. (Courtesy US Mint.)

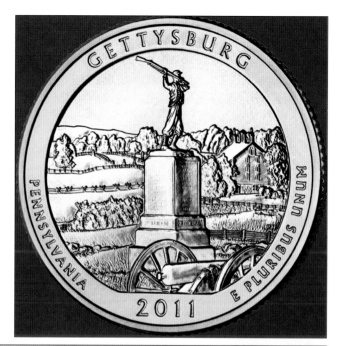

During the August 2010 restoration of the New York State Monument in Soldiers' National Cemetery, the author was granted the opportunity to ascend over the burial grounds in a crane. Because the tombstones of the 3,512 Civil War soldiers buried here were made level with the ground in the 1940s, one cannot obtain a holistic view of the markers unless hovering above them. (Author's collection.)

A staple of park operations is interpretive park ranger tours. At the height of the summer season, the park offers over 20 free programs each day. Energetic park ranger Jacob Dinkelaker is seen here delivering a "Sunset on Little Round" tour in July 2010. (Author's collection.)

A popular ranger presentation is the evening campfire program at the amphitheater on West Confederate Avenue. Staff members share episodes of Civil War history in the same flavor as traditional nature talks in western parks. In this August 2011 image, park ranger Aaron Urbanski prepares a roaring bonfire for his interactive program. (Author's collection.)

Since 1915, dedicated licensed battlefield guides have dutifully counseled visitors with comprehensive battlefield tours. Typically offering rental tours two hours in length, guides are officially licensed to provide tours by the National Park Service following rigorous examinations. Guide Rich Kohr is seen here orienting students with the People to People Student Ambassador Program. (Courtesy Bill Dowling.)

The park's living historian, Bill Fean, offers a personalized tour of Soldiers' National Cemetery to visitors in the summer of 2012. Unlike park ranger programs, these vignettes are performed in character. Fean was portraying James Sullivan of the 6th Wisconsin Infantry at the grave of James Kelly, who was mortally wounded on July 1, 1863. (Courtesy GNMP.)

Poised defiantly 110 feet above the ground atop the dome of the Pennsylvania Memorial is a statue of Athena Nike—the goddess of victory. The 7,500-pound figure was sculpted by artist Samuel Murray and was cast with the bronze of Civil War cannon. Dedicated in 1910, the Pennsylvania Memorial bears the names of 34,000 Pennsylvanians who participated in the Gettysburg Campaign. (Author's collection.)

A favorite landmark among visitors is Devil's Den. The 200-million-year-old igneous rock outcropping witnessed heavy combat on July 2, 1863, as Confederates chaotically advanced toward Little Round Top. Here, ranger Matt Atkinson greets a little rebel next to the guns of the 4th New York Independent Battery. The large oak tree offering shade is one of the park's seven confirmed "Witness Trees" that were alive in 1863. (Courtesy GNMP.)

America's transportation revolutions are often reflected by the means in which tourists explore the park. Beginning in the late 2000s, Segway tours gained popularity among visitors seeking new perspective of the battleground. In this photograph, a licensed battlefield guide brings up the rear on a Segway tour heading down Wheatfield Road. (Courtesy GNMP.)

On November 19, 2012, filmmaker Steven Spielberg delivered the keynote speech for Dedication Day. Spielberg's arrival coincided with the release of his Academy Award–winning movie *Lincoln*. Spielberg said to the crowd of 10,000, "I've never stood any place on earth where it's easier to be humble than here. Gettysburg. Delivering an *address*." (Author's collection.)

Police officers and first responders of the South Central Task Force hold a drill exercise at the base of Little Round Top in May 2013. The task force consists of law enforcement from eight counties in southern Pennsylvania who facilitate emergency prevention, response, and recovery. The battlefield serves as a training ground for police as well as the military. (Courtesy GNMP.)

Gettysburg's annual Memorial Day parade is a spring favorite among locals and visitors alike. The procession rolls up Baltimore Street and concludes in the Soldiers' National Cemetery. This timeline of living historians depicting American conflicts serves as visual testimony to Gettysburg as the reenactor capital of the nation. (Author's collection.)

Following the annual Memorial Day parade, a diverse crowd of visitors pours into Soldiers' National Cemetery to participate in the subsequent ceremony, offering a stirring scene of patriotism and historical awareness, as seen here in 2013. (Author's collection.)

As is customary of Memorial Day ceremonies, students from nearby elementary schools place flags at the tombstones in Soldiers' National Cemetery. The young man here wanders through the Unknown section of the hallowed graveyard. Over 900 unidentified soldiers rest in eternal anonymity at Gettysburg. (Courtesy Lynn Light Heller.)

Ken Burns, director of the acclaimed series *The Civil War*, speaks with a news crew on the 2013 anniversary of Lincoln's speech. That same year, Burns filmed part of his production *The Address* in the park. The documentary focuses on Vermont students with learning disabilities who demonstrate great courage in their attempts to comprehend and publicly deliver the Gettysburg Address to peers and family. (Courtesy Lynn Light Heller.)

Booming park visitation in the 1990s spurred an expectation for a higher degree of authenticity. Modern intrusions such as private homes, motels, restaurants, and telephone lines—as seen here on the Emmitsburg Road—detracted from the immersion visitors desired. Beginning in the new millennium, the National Park Service fully intended to grant the public its wish. In a matter of years, these utility lines would be gone. (Courtesy GNMP.)

Three

CHANGES IN THE LAND

The July 4, 2000, demolition of the Gettysburg National Tower marked a symbolic moment in battlefield reclamation. Long considered an eyesore by historical purists, the privately owned tower was acquired by the government via eminent domain, with $3 million in compensation granted to the owners. Richard Moe of the National Trust for Historic Preservation said in an interview, "To a preservationist, demolition is almost always an ugly word. But not today. Today, we're doing something right." (Courtesy GNMP.)

Completed in 1974, the Gettysburg National Tower was built by real estate magnate Thomas Ottenstein, who envisioned his creation as a "Classroom in the Sky." While the tower offered a sublime view of the battlefield, historians considered the Space Needle–like structure an obtrusive monument to money. Despite efforts by the commonwealth and park to prohibit its erection, the tower stood as a tourist attraction for 26 years. (Courtesy GNMP.)

An infamous "land swap" between GNMP and Gettysburg College in 1990 initiated national scandal. The college traded a portion of its athletic fields in exchange for access to this historic railroad cut so a rail line crossing the campus could be diverted. The ensuing excavation of this significant battleground feature pushed history advocates to call for congressional investigation, but the irrevocable damage had already been done. (Courtesy GNMP.)

One not need look far beyond the boundaries of the park to discover memorials. This statue of heroine Elizabeth Thorn was dedicated in Evergreen Cemetery in November 2002. Six months pregnant in July 1863, Thorn personally buried some 100 Union dead. The monument honors all women who contributed to the Civil War. (Courtesy Lynn Light Heller.)

Appointed superintendent in 1994, John Lastschar (right) emerged as one of the most important figures in Gettysburg's progression. He initiated a revolutionary 1997 General Management Plan proposing landscape restoration and new visitor facilities. Despite his reassignment amid controversy in 2009, his audacious vision for the park has been enjoyed by millions since. He is seen here in 2005 with Friends of the National Parks at Gettysburg director David Booz. (Courtesy GNMP.)

The benefits of battlefield landscape restoration are conveyed through these before and after photographs of the 1st Minnesota Infantry monument. Prior to restoration, visitors here could hardly comprehend troop movements due to heavy tree growth in the Codori-Trostle Thicket. With tree removal, vistas closely resembling those of 1863 reappeared. According to the NPS, this ongoing restoration project "includes the replacement of historic fence lines, orchards, and farm lanes as well as the return of grasslands, farmlands, orchards and woodlands that played important roles in the battle." (Both, courtesy GNMP.)

National parks are notoriously underfunded by the federal government. Therefore, parks depend heavily on spirited volunteers. On October 8, 2010, nearly 100 personnel from Dover Air Force Base contributed 400 hours realigning World War II–era headstones in Soldiers' National Cemetery. Sgt. Tammy Hintz commented, "It brings satisfaction to know we have helped preserve and protect this national treasure." (Courtesy GNMP.)

Not all visitors are concerned with the well being of historic resources. On the night of February 16, 2006, vandals dislodged the cannoneer statue of Smith's 4th New York Battery atop Devil's Den, dragging it 162 feet by car, stealing its head, and inflicting tens of thousands of dollars in damage. (Courtesy GNMP.)

That same night, vandals also struck the 114th Pennsylvania Infantry monument near the Emmitsburg Road. The iconic saber-wielding arm of the 11th Massachusetts Infantry monument was also ripped from its pedestal. Here, ranger Laurie Gantz surveys the damage. The perpetrators were never apprehended. As the desecrations made national headlines, park staff embarked on the arduous repair process. (Courtesy GNMP.)

Restoration of the 4th New York Artillery monument was a five-year process. Because the memorial's bronze head was missing, park staff searched for an identical copy to create a mold. Fortunately, an exact version of the statue stood in Manchester, New Hampshire. "That was about as lucky as you can imagine," said park specialist Brian Griffin, pictured here with the new mold. (Courtesy GNMP.)

On November 28, 2011, the restored 4th New York artillerist was resurrected atop his perch in Devil's Den. Ranger Chuck Teague was quoted in an *Evening Sun* article as saying, "The thrill is in overcoming the tragedy of what happened here." (Courtesy Lynn Light Heller.)

Gettysburg farmer Peter Frey lived comfortably on this piece of property until his barn became a II Corps field hospital in 1863. During the July 3 bombardment, the farm endured intense artillery fire, which shattered the house roof. Sadly, this scenario was partially re-created when a fire engulfed the structure on April 27, 2007. Sprinklers saved the home and possibly the family residing therein. (Courtesy GNMP.)

Gettysburg businessman David LeVan twice campaigned to build a casino within cannon shot of GNMP. Here, members of "No Casino Gettysburg" rally behind Peter Gaytan of the American Legion at the state capitol on September 21, 2010. Gaytan noted, "The history of the country is a national issue." All Gettysburg casino proposals were rejected by the commonwealth. (Courtesy Civil War Trust.)

Volunteers replant peach trees on the former Joseph Sherfy property. Landscape restoration was not without controversy. Just as many trees were cut as planted in order to re-create historic vistas. In addition, the park's over-populated deer herd was "trimmed" by several hundred. For some, the destruction of woodlots and the killing of wildlife seemed antithetical to the mission of the National Park Service. (Courtesy GNMP.)

In partnership with the Gettysburg Foundation in 2008, some 72 peach trees were planted on the former Sherfy Farm property. By 2012, nearly 3,000 apple trees on 35 different historic orchard sites were planted to create an authentic 1860s agrarian environment. (Courtesy Lynn Light Heller.)

Coinciding with ongoing landscape restoration was the mammoth undertaking of preserving and reviving the historic 1884 cyclorama painting representing Pickett's Charge. Beginning in 2003, extensive conservation work unfolded as the six-ton canvas was prepared for its new home. (Courtesy GNMP.)

A century's worth of public exhibition, improper storage, misguided restorations, water damage, and incorrect mounting in multiple facilities left the once majestic "Battle of Gettysburg" cyclorama a shadow of its former self. Slashed, trimmed, and buckled over the years, the painting's $15 million restoration came not a moment too soon. (Courtesy GNMP.)

In September 2009, the Gettysburg cyclorama was vividly reborn following a six-year restoration. Missing panels were re-created, a three-dimensional foreground with debris was reconstructed, and the canvas's original hyperbolic shape was reincorporated. A dramatic audiovisual program narrated by Glenn Close enlightens visitors who view the painting from an elevated platform. (Courtesy Bill Dowling.)

The Gettysburg cyclorama's latest home is the Gettysburg National Military Park Museum and Visitor Center, seen here in an architect's rendering. The park was in need of new museum facilities to accommodate nearly two million annual visitors. Unlike previous park installations, this one was not built on core battlefield and closer resembled farming structures. As *USA Today* observed, "The complex is a red and gray stone structure reminiscent of a 19th-century barn and covering the equivalent of 2 ½ football fields. It is tucked into a wooded area on the Gettysburg National Military Park—land that saw no major action in the three-day Civil War battle." (Courtesy GNMP.)

Construction on the new visitor center began in 2006, with costs totaling more than $100 million. Assisting with fundraising was the Gettysburg Foundation, the park's nonprofit partner. This collaboration has fostered a unique power dynamic within the park. The 139,000-square-foot facility is owned by the foundation but concurrently serves as the base of operations for the ranger staff. (Courtesy GNMP.)

Park ranger Tom Holbrook ceremoniously conducts the final lockup of the old park visitor center on April 13, 2008. The 30-by-30-foot Electric Map inside was sold to businessman Scott Roland via a government auction for $14,000 in September 2012 with the intention of making it a private attraction in nearby Hanover. (Courtesy GNMP.)

The formal opening of the new visitor center was celebrated on September 26, 2008, upon the completion of the cyclorama restoration. From left to right are volunteers Joan and Art Pore, Gettysburg Foundation vice president Elliot Gruber, deputy superintendent John McKenna, and Barbara Finfrock participating in the ribbon cutting. The *Washington Post* editorialized that the park "is undergoing the most radical change to its look and feel in a generation." (Courtesy GNMP.)

The opening of the new visitor center was not without quarrel. Some argued the Gettysburg Foundation possessed too much power in operations while a handful was less than impressed with the museum. Older tourists missed the endless rows of muskets, while pro-Confederate visitors were offended by the incorporation of slavery into exhibits. Regardless, the park now had a museum that offered a comprehensive overview of the Civil War. (Courtesy GNMP.)

Known as a storyline museum, the visitor center's Gettysburg Museum of the American Civil War interweaves artifacts, photographs, and multimedia to contextualize Gettysburg within the broader narrative of America's deadliest conflict. Museum admission was originally free, but monetary shortfalls in initial months reversed that option. Above, museum technician Andrew Newman makes exhibit adjustments. (Courtesy GNMP.)

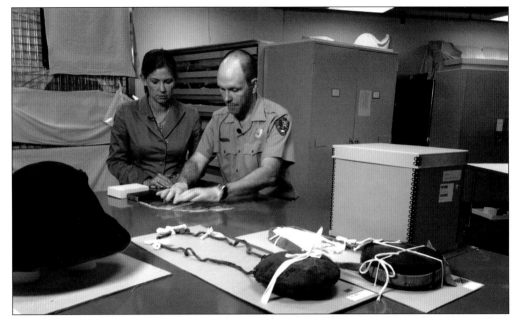

Beneath Gettysburg's vast museum complex is one of the richest repositories of Civil War relics. As per standard museum practice, only a small percentage of total artifacts are displayed at any one time. The park cares for some one million items. Curator Greg Goodell is seen here describing artifacts to CBS reporter Jan Crawford in June 2013. The battle-scarred hat of Gen. Abner Doubleday sits in the foreground. (Courtesy GNMP.)

The park expanded into downtown Gettysburg by opening the David Wills House in time for the February 2009 Lincoln bicentennial. Wills was a local Republican attorney who hosted Lincoln the night prior to the delivery of the Gettysburg Address. The statue outside depicts Lincoln greeting a modern tourist who is endearingly called "Perry Como" by locals. (Courtesy GNMP.)

Throughout March 2009, the old visitor center, along Taneytown Road, was demolished in the name of landscape restoration. While many park guests were pleased by such progressions, some nostalgic visitors yearned for the days of the quaint, homespun museum. Touring this area of the battlefield today, one is hard-pressed to recognize this building even existed. (Courtesy GNMP.)

Beginning in 2009, the dilapidated William Patterson cabin behind Cemetery Ridge was completely disassembled and meticulously reconstructed. With portions of the home dating to the 1790s, the structure is the oldest within park boundaries. During the battle, the home was utilized as a temporary aid station for the Union's II Corps. (Courtesy GNMP.)

Located only feet away from a sharp curve along West Howard Avenue, the 74th Pennsylvania Infantry monument became victim to speeding drivers on multiple occasions. The worst of these collisions occurred on November 14, 2003, when an SUV shattered the stone memorial. Within a year, the monument was back in place—only to be struck and repaired again in 2010. (Barb Adams photograph; courtesy GNMP.)

Dedicated volunteers contribute various talents to the educational mission of the park. Volunteer Bill Aldrich donated some 2,000 hours over the course of six months throughout 2010 and 2011 to create a model of downtown Gettysburg as it appeared in 1863. The 48-by-69-inch model includes 260 buildings and is on display on the first floor of the David Wills House. (Courtesy GNMP.)

Park maintenance staff member Bob Jones was treated to a rare surprise at work on August 4, 2011. Following the collapse of a large oak tree on Culp's Hill during a summer storm, Jones's chain saw was subsequently caught on two Civil War bullets embedded in the wood. The portions of trunk were soon after taken to the park museum for preservation. (Courtesy GNMP.)

Vandals struck Gettysburg again on February 29, 2012, as obscenities were spray painted on the 2nd Andrews Sharpshooters monument on Sickles Avenue. Preservation supervisor Lucas Flickinger, pictured here, had the monument cleaned within one day. Flickinger later received a 2013 NPS stewardship award for his efforts, including the restoration of some 500 cannon and monuments that year. (Courtesy GNMP.)

The nonprofit Civil War Trust has sponsored Park Day since 1996. The annual spring event takes place at dozens of battlefields across the country, and volunteers paint cannon, clear brush, and assist in general maintenance of historical landmarks. Enthused volunteers are seen here in 2012 at the rocky base of Little Round Top. (Courtesy GNMP.)

Preservationist Luke Harmon cleans the bronze statue of Pennsylvania governor Andrew Curtin on the Pennsylvania Memorial during the summer of 2012. Curtin was a staunch political ally of President Lincoln and was one of the moving forces behind the creation of Gettysburg's Soldiers' National Cemetery, hence his prominent place on the memorial's front. (Author's collection.)

Monument preservation mason Gary Currens repairs the 140th New York Infantry monument on Little Round Top. Depicted on the memorial is 26-year-old Patrick O'Rorke, who was mortally struck in the neck by an enemy bullet near this spot. Despite O'Rorke's misfortunes, many visitors rub the monument's nose for some "luck of the Irish." The seemingly harmless tradition actually deteriorates the bronze. (Courtesy GNMP.)

Some park visitors donate heirlooms and prized relics to be preserved for posterity. Attorney Craig Bashein (center) donated a vast collection of artifacts to the park in December 2012, including personal items of Generals Philip Sheridan and Alexander Webb. Here, Supt. Bob Kirby (left) and historian Scott Hartwig (right) examine a battlefield map created by Capt. J.D. Briscoe of Gen. David Birney's staff. (Courtesy GNMP.)

The former Cyclorama Center in Zeigler's Grove sat vacant for five years following the 2008 opening of the new visitor center. The planned demolition of the inadequate structure was delayed when friends and family of the building's architect, Richard Neutra, filed claims that the NPS did not properly examine alternatives for the facility. Despite numerous legal hurdles, the center's walls fell in March 2013. (Courtesy Bill Dowling.)

The close proximity of public lands and private enterprise has long resulted in interesting dynamics in Gettysburg. In the summer of 2014, the newly refurbished Gettysburg Heritage Center offered aerial tours in a balloon similar in style to the Civil War's *Intrepid*. Ranger Bert Barnett is shown giving a tour in Soldiers' National Cemetery as the balloon hovers nearby. (Courtesy GNMP.)

On October 7, 2014, park staff oversaw a controlled burn along Hancock Avenue. According to the park, such strategies are implemented to perpetuate the open character of the landscape, maintain habitats, and limit invasive species. Such burns offer a surreal, smoky aura to the battlefield, reminiscent of Civil War combat. (Courtesy GNMP.)

While fresh methods of historical interpretation developed within the park, such was also the case in the town of Gettysburg itself. New reflections upon the 1863 civilian experience play out at sites like the Shriver House Museum, shown here on Baltimore Street. (Author's collection.)

The 1858 Gettysburg Train Station witnessed horrors as a Civil War hospital, greeted Abraham Lincoln, and serviced aged veterans upon their return for reunions. For years, the station sat vacant until it was converted into a visitor contact station. In November 2014, the center was repainted from its vibrant 1880s gold hue to its more subdued gray and brown tone of the 1860s. (Courtesy Gettysburg Foundation.)

Over 1,000 spectators convened at the Pennsylvania Memorial on April 30, 2011, to mark the opening of the Civil War sesquicentennial. Supt. Bob Kirby (at podium) encouraged visitors to bring young people to the park. Planning was already under way for the battle's 150th anniversary in 2013. (Courtesy GNMP.)

Four

150 Years Later

Every May, the interpretive staff of Gettysburg's two parks celebrates the onset of the summer season with a barbecue at Eisenhower National Historic Site. Comprised of young interns, seasonal rangers, and veteran staff, these select few individuals guide tens of thousands of visitors every year. This May 2013 photograph shows staff re-creating the iconic "pointing ranger" image in anticipation of the battle's sesquicentennial. (Author's collection.)

Thousands of spectators poured into the area behind Leister Farm on June 30, 2013, for the official opening of the Battle of Gettysburg's 150th anniversary. Country music star Trace Adkins (pictured) performed the national anthem. Later, author Doris Kearns Goodwin delivered the keynote address. The evening concluded with a moving luminaria in Soldiers' National Cemetery. (Courtesy GNMP.)

Rangers performed dozens of programs every day throughout the battle's 150th anniversary. One of the most widely attended tours was entitled "Last March of the Iron Brigade." Led by rangers Scott Hartwig and Dan Welch, the group of over 1,000 visitors and reenactors traced the route of the acclaimed Midwestern soldiers as they deployed into battle. (Courtesy GNMP.)

Coinciding with the battle's sesquicentennial was the opening of the Seminary Ridge Museum in the former Lutheran Theological Seminary. Seen here from the vicinity of the Herbst Woods, the structure served as an observation platform and field hospital for both sides. The interactive museum chronicles the battle juxtaposed with the religious and social issues of the 1860s. (Buddy Secor photograph; courtesy GNMP.)

Ranger Jim Flook speaks to the masses on July 2, 2013, as visitors converge on Devil's Den. To lessen traffic congestion on battlefield roads, the park partnered with regional shuttle services to ensure a steady flow of travel. As many as 25,000 people visited the park each day during the week of the anniversary. (Courtesy GNMP.)

A sense of camaraderie pervaded during the 150th anniversary. Licensed battlefield guides Garry Adelman and Tim Smith delivered a program at the Rose Farm, providing 3D glasses to 500 attendees to view the Alexander Gardner photographs taken there in 1863. Adelman later reflected of the anniversary, "[P]eople were happy, pensive, and engaged. I have never seen anything like it in my 19 years as a Gettysburg guide." (Buddy Secor photograph; courtesy GNMP.)

In a moment of near-mystical symbolism, a double rainbow emerged over the Gettysburg Battlefield on the evening of July 2, 2013, stretching almost the exact length of the Union lines from Culp's Hill to Little Round Top. (Buddy Secor photograph; courtesy GNMP.)

Dedicated in a time of national reconciliation during World War I, the impressive Virginia Memorial on West Confederate Avenue features stoic representations of Robert E. Lee and Virginia soldiers. Taken on July 2, 2013, this photograph exhibits the ironic serenity one can find on the battlefield at night. (Buddy Secor photograph; courtesy GNMP.)

Throngs of visitors flooded into the park museum in July 2013. One notable highlight included a temporary exhibit entitled Treasures of the Civil War. Featuring mementos from 13 celebrated Civil War personalities, the exhibition included Ulysses Grant's sword and a lock of Robert E. Lee's hair. (Courtesy GNMP.)

ELIZABETH THORN
SOLDIER'S WIFE AND CEMETERY CARETAKER

Elizabeth Thorn was a German immigrant living in the gatehouse of the local cemetery and caring for that cemetery, her aging parents, and her young children while her husband was at war. This gatehouse would become a general's headquarters as well as a hospital while she fled south to safety. She wrote: "When I left home, I had put on a heavier dress than usual . . . I lived in that dress for six weeks." Elizabeth and her father buried 105 bodies in the cemetery in the hot, humid July heat; she was six months pregnant at the time.

Stand in Elizabeth's footsteps in front of the gatehouse that was her home, next to the Baltimore Street entrance of the Soldiers' National Cemetery.

Photo courtesy of Evergreen Cemetery Association.

As an educational outreach tool, the park issued collector cards reminiscent of ambrotype photograph cases of the Civil War era. Each card featured a personal story of an individual who experienced the battle. Young visitors were encouraged to follow in the footsteps of these personalities. (Courtesy GNMP/Evergreen Cemetery Association.)

Living history demonstrations were a popular component of the 150th anniversary. Union reenactors bivouacked near the Pennsylvania Memorial, while Confederate reenactors encamped in Pitzer Woods. At 1:00 p.m. on July 3, artillery on both sides of the battlefield fired every 10 minutes to represent the 1863 cannon duel. Here, scores of visitors amass to photograph the cannonade. (Buddy Secor photograph; courtesy GNMP.)

Some 15,000 visitors congregated on Seminary Ridge to re-create Pickett's Charge. Ranger Troy Harman initiated the "rebel yell," and soon after, the entire ridgeline was swept up by the Confederate battle cry. As a final cannon volley ignited at 3:00 p.m., the pack of history enthusiasts embarked upon the trek across the open landscape. (Courtesy GNMP.)

Over 25,000 spectators assembled on Cemetery Ridge to view fellow visitors re-create the fateful July 3rd assault. As the two vast lines converged, all halted while "Echo Taps" played. As journalist Donald Gilliland wrote of the moment, "It only lasted a few moments, the playing of "Taps," but in those few moments tens of thousands of people thought about something other than themselves." (Courtesy GNMP.)

A young visitor captures the spirit of the 72nd Pennsylvania Infantry monument at the Angle. The statue was toppled by a windstorm a week prior, bending the bronze rifle stock. Few visitors noticed amidst the excitement of the day. As one tourist was quoted in *USA Today*, "This is where it all changed. This is where we came back to be a real United States again." (Courtesy GNMP.)

Confederate reenactors take a pause after the playing of "Taps" on Cemetery Ridge. While part of the proceedings exhibited pageantry, writers such as Tony Horwitz urged Americans to see "the inglorious reality of Civil War combat" rather than be captivated by its romanticization. Horwitz also noted that Civil War commemorations remind people that the "struggle for racial justice, and for national cohesion, continues still." (Buddy Secor photograph; courtesy GNMP.)

A southern reenactor peers across the fields of Pickett's Charge in a scene noticeably lacking modern intrusions on July 3, 2013. Even on its busiest days, the battlefield is serene in contrast to the pandemonium of battle. (Courtesy GNMP.)

An after-action assessment of the anniversary takes place in the park's Reading Room on the evening of July 3, 2013. Staff from other Civil War battlefields, including Appomattox, Fredericksburg and Spotsylvania, Harpers Ferry, Petersburg, and Richmond, aided in the commemoration. (Courtesy Jim Flook.)

The sesquicentennial was a true collaborative effort among the various branches of the park. Here, park law enforcement re-creates a Civil War–style photograph at General Meade's headquarters. Pictured are, from left to right, (first row) John Clark III, Maria Brady, Seth Goodspeed, and Anne Petersen; (second row, on the porch) Steve Wukovitz, John Sherman, Doug Murphy, Ryan Levins, Eric Pelletier, Clint Burkholder, Morgan Brooks, and Brian Hogan. (Courtesy GNMP).

In September 2013, the Congressional Medal of Honor Society held its convention at Gettysburg. For the ceremonial concert at the Pennsylvania Memorial, Supt. Bob Kirby waived the long-standing policy of not allowing fireworks in the park. One year later, Lt. Alonzo Cushing became the 64th Medal of Honor recipient from the battle when posthumously awarded by Pres. Barack Obama. (Author's collection.)

One week after the 2013 Medal of Honor convention, some 3,000 Boy Scouts descended upon the battlefield for a massive jamboree. Hiking the trails and assisting with landscape restoration by day, the youth camped at the George Spangler Farm by night. (Courtesy GNMP.)

For the thousands of Boy Scouts visiting Gettysburg in September 2013, rangers were posted at various stations to conduct interpretive programs for rotating groups. Above, ranger Casimer Rosiecki converses with a troop leader as Scouts settle for lunch at the visitor center. (Author's collection.)

National media poured into Gettysburg in anticipation of the 150th anniversary of the Gettysburg Address. In this scene, NBC's Harry Smith interviews park historian John Heiser at the Angle for a special segment of *Meet the Press*. (Courtesy GNMP.)

To mark the anniversary of Lincoln's arrival in Gettysburg, the David Wills House hosted special evening hours on November 18, 2013. Ranger John Hoptak oriented visitors through the structure 150 years to the hour that the 16th president completed his Gettysburg Address in this room. (Author's collection.)

November 19, 2013, was a crisp autumn day as thousands lined the gates of Soldiers' National Cemetery to mark the sesquicentennial of Lincoln's acclaimed address. This vivid photograph captures the beauty and painful grandeur of the Union burial ground. (Buddy Secor photograph; courtesy GNMP.)

Lincoln impersonator James Getty (1932–2015) shakes hands with celebrated Civil War historian James McPherson, who served as the keynote speaker at the Gettysburg Address sesquicentennial. McPherson commented in his remarks, "The Battle of Gettysburg became the hinge of fate on which turned the destiny of the nation and its new birth of freedom." (Buddy Secor photograph; courtesy GNMP.)

A seemingly countless number of Lincoln portrayers roamed the grounds of Soldiers' National Cemetery throughout the 150th anniversary observances. Here, a young visitor is thrilled to acquire the autograph of "Mr. Lincoln." (Tami Heilemann photograph; courtesy GNMP.)

Ranger Morgan Brooks read a proclamation by President Obama marking the anniversary of the Gettysburg Address. The statement noted, "The trajectory of our history should give us hope . . . [that] this nation, under God, shall remain the last, best hope of Earth." Despite the poetic nature of the speech, many were disappointed with Obama's conspicuous absence. Justice Antonin Scalia is seen in the background. (Courtesy GNMP.)

The Saturday closest to the November 19th anniversary of the Gettysburg Address is known as Remembrance Day. On that evening every year, the 3,512 graves of the Union dead are saluted with an evocative luminaria, with each candle symbolizing a lost life. (Courtesy Bill Dowling.)

Battle anniversaries are bustling times regardless of their numerical designations. Ranger John Hoptak leads a July 1, 2014, "Battlewalk" from Oak Hill to Oak Ridge as period-attired intern Brandon Benner (foreground) brings up the rear. (Courtesy GNMP.)

Civil War Trust president James Lighthizer offers remarks on July 1, 2014, as historians celebrated the organization's purchase of Robert E. Lee's former headquarters for $5.5 million. The four-acre tract of real estate also included an adjoining Quality Inn and pub to be demolished in the name of historical preservation. (Courtesy Civil War Trust.)

Every September, convoys of World War II vehicles whiz through the battlefield as the neighboring Eisenhower National Historic Site celebrates its annual World War II Weekend. Here, from left to right, reenactors Mike Carper, Andrew Collins, John Heiser, and Mark Frederick take a break at the Pennsylvania Memorial in 2014. (Author's collection.)

The Association of Licensed Battlefield Guides celebrated its 100th anniversary in 2015. Consisting of over 150 authorized guides, these ladies and gentlemen are a favorite resource among visitors. The guides still abide by their century-old motto: "A Good Battlefield Trip is the Best Advertisement for Gettysburg." (Courtesy Bill Dowling.)

The George Spangler property flooded with some 1,900 wounded following the three-day clash. Purchased by the Gettysburg Foundation in 2008, the property opened for summer tours in 2013. Here, ranger Philip Brown delivers a presentation on site the following summer. Park spokeswoman Katie Lawhon commented of the landmark, "It's something fresh, and you really get a sense of the importance of it." (Courtesy GNMP.)

A summertime tradition at Gettysburg is living history programming. Offering visitors the means to better visualize Civil War combatants, reenactors present various learning opportunities. In this scene, Confederate artillerists conduct a demonstration near Pitzer's Woods. (Courtesy GNMP.)

Following the racially driven murders of nine churchgoers in Charleston, South Carolina, in June 2015, GNMP pulled select pieces of potentially offensive Confederate flag merchandise from the park bookstore. Original Confederate flags in the museum remained on display. The shootings and the subsequent removal of Confederate imagery from public spaces throughout the country reignited a fiery social debate about the Civil War and its unsavory legacies. (Courtesy GNMP.)

An early morning fog hovers over the Valley of Death and before the 155th Pennsylvania Infantry monument on Little Round Top. Gettysburg National Military Park has long served as a platform for debate and discovery among the American people. The battlefield's pristine landscape stands not only as a testament to soldiers of 1863, but also to subsequent generations who preserve it for those who follow. (Courtesy Lynn Light Heller.)

DISCOVER THOUSANDS OF LOCAL HISTORY BOOKS FEATURING MILLIONS OF VINTAGE IMAGES

Arcadia Publishing, the leading local history publisher in the United States, is committed to making history accessible and meaningful through publishing books that celebrate and preserve the heritage of America's people and places.

Find more books like this at
www.arcadiapublishing.com

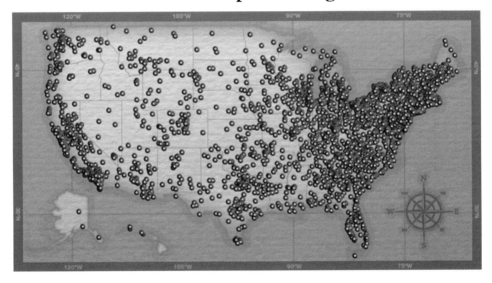

Search for your hometown history, your old stomping grounds, and even your favorite sports team.